A Slice of Life

Written by, Alishba Javed

Dedicated to the person who inspired, and encouraged me to write, Mrs. Anna Desjardins.

With thanks to, my mother, Nosheen, and my father, Younus.

Table of Contents

Cake

Everything in life

Whisked together

And baked

In a glorious cake

Friends

Love

Sad

Bad

Overlooked

And Metaphors

...

Problem

I've got a problem that's insane

That I can't understand my brain

If I'm in pain I don't know why

And it just seems that I lie,

To me...

The Island Of Castaway

On a medium sized island in the Bermuda triangle there lived a village of castaways.

A town of people who washed upon a shore.

They all lived a happy life, and spoke many languages. A plethora of cultures lived on the island, castaways come from many places

The place a world of its own, not all like ours at all. For you see the citizens were at peace. Sure they squabbled and bickered, but war stayed in, and battle was never called. They all had been on the same boat, the one that sank.

On the island of castaway, everyone always chatted, for what else could they do they had nothing to stay glued too.

They strolled across the shore with someone they loved

They went out to sea to catch some grub.

On the island of castaway no one committed crime, for what was there to steal? When was there time? Currency didn't exist, no leader to jeopardize. Who would you kill? , everyone was just trying to survive. There was always something to do, no time for the luxury of hate.

On the island of castaway emotions are understood. Feeling sadness and fear aren't thought to be signs of weakness...they're not shunned. The people often grieve over those who didn't make it to the island, those who no longer are.

The island of castaway may be a small island...of grief, sadness, and also isolated, but it is the best place to be

An island of relative peace

Words

Some people's words are stuck on with glue

Carved into a grave

A building which is hurricane proof,

Stuck there to stay.

Others words are paper Mache

Words that decay,

Written in chalk

At any moment can wash away.

True Love

True love is a rose

It is beautiful and sweet

Alas it has its thorns

But it shall not be gone,

Till it withers away.

Windshield

The vehicles glass being the eye,

Covered with the tears of the sky,

The vision of the rider blurred,

Till the sunlight hits the earth,

And you can see again.

Money

Paper that we give such value,

Paper that we sacrifice much for,

For that paper has not much value

, Outside of society's doors.

Plane

The large chunk of metal

Seeming too heavy to fly

Yet it reaches the sky

Arms spread wide,

Whizzing by.

Third Wheel

They're a vehicle that changes over time.

A group of three,

As happy as can be.

Then he says he is in love with thee.

And you are pushed at the edge of a circle

That used to be big enough to fit you all in.

For now it is a box too small to fit you all in.

They deny, saying the circle is plenty big.

That nothing will change.

Truth is though that your tricycle,

Has become a bicycle.

World

You start with just your home,

 Just you and yourself alone.

Then you have community,

 More people and places to see.

Then you gain the city,

 A small world where you roam free.

Then you gain a country so many sights,

So close to you, yet not seen.

Then you see the world.

So big and overwhelming.

 So many people to meet.

 So many that you will never know.

 Too much to take in all at once.

 So you start with step one.

I Wish

I wish that the world was less strange.

That we wouldn't gain rage over game.

That our emotions weren't seen as a charade.

That serious issues and blame weren't seen as humor

 For that is a shame.

That we would not judge all,

While only knowing one.

 For we obsess over our petty troubles

 Not realizing that the world's problems,

Have just begun.

Orange

Life is an orange

Some see it sweet

And others see it sour

 But it is always a bit of both

Opportunity

Those who do not see what is right in front of their nose are in a horror movie.

Missing the chance to open the door and run away.

So they die.

Book

All you see are paper and ink,

Or at least that is what you think,

For truly you see another person,

View, thoughts and feeling,

What they hear,

What they are dreaming.

Another life to live

 That's what a book is.

Time

Laying on the ground,

Watching the clouds fly away,

, As time ticks away.

Sitting on a bench,

Watching trees sway,

, As time ticks away.

Watching a film

On a chilly day,

, As time ticks away.

Staring at the ceiling,

Alone on your bed,

You do this everyday

...As time ticks away.

This is why they say,

Make the most of everyday,

Because, everyday,

Time ticks away.

Holding your tongue

Hi what's up he wrote

But what could've come before

Could it have been a romantic poem?

Maybe a song yet to be sung?

A note from a royal king?

Or someone shady?

Or a list of confessions?

Maybe a sad note?

A secret dream unknown?

But what am I to persist

Since backspace seems to be the computers way of holding your tongue.

Ice in mud

One of clear beauty

The other of opaque sludge

One chilling and dazzling

The other mushy lumps

But, together a strange mix of beauty and disgust,

Overall beautiful.

Outlaw

Looking society in the face

Although they say you're a disgrace

Serving restrictions on a dish

But you do as you wish

Jumped the fence

Freedom is right in front of my face

But if I take it they shall say I am a disgrace,

Just a hop and a skip away,

Freedom for the rest of the day,

But what is there after I make the faithful leap,

What is there to do once all is mine to take?

What shall I do at the end of the day?

All I know is mine to keep,

I took the freedom for whatever it was worth.

Hence,

That's why I jumped the fence.

Wanderlust

All I want is to go to a place I've never known

Be anywhere except home

Find other places to love

I'd gladly give up all I have to go to another place

I'm not asking to go to space

Just to be anywhere but here

To have the time to relax and be glad

To be able to move away whenever I feel

Bored

I'm not a rock I'm wind

I move where I wish weather you want me to or not

No matter how much you want old

All I want is new

New for me

Old for you

To be in a surging sea of humanity or

A calm sea of none

This desire I trust

Wanderlust...

Great loss

Seemingly polar opposites

But in the same place

One can't stop grinning

They've wiped the smirk of the others face

One celebrating, making a mess

The other cleaning up their own

They both have great loss

Of those they love

But one gained great victory

And the other lost to the rest of the world

Sister

She eats them all

So I can have none

She frames me so well

Broken china her gun

Takes all my clothes

Never asked

(Not even once)

And the torture has just begun

I can trust her with nothing

She'll tell everyone

They say she's a good girl

I say she spits out lies

(I bet she could convince them that she flies)

Around her I've always got the blues

(Not to mention she ruined my favorite shoes)

But even though the way she plays the role of good girl makes me want to hurl

I love her more than anything else in the world

Emotion

You paint the canvas of your eyes

With paint from your mind

Shaded by what surrounds you

Changed colors bring

Things

Of worry

And joy

Of those who see you as a toy

Some paint difficult to remove

Is painted over

And over

Until it slowly fades away

Perhaps to come again

Another day

Boredom

Refusing to

Sleep

To eat

To go outside

To watch TV

To go and make it snow

To put on a show

To cook

And

To clean

To save a damsel in distress

To put on a wedding dress

To take pictures of fawn

To dance with prawn

To see who has the longest yawn

No

You just do nothing

Alone

Alone

At home

Alone

At work

Alone

At a party

Alone

On earth

Mentally

Lonely

At a party

Lonely

Getting coffee

Lonely

At work

Lonely

Anywhere you can be lonely,

But not really alone.

Friends

The one who doesn't mind you invading their personal space

The one who you'll let trash your place

The one who knows you

Sweet and sour

The one that knows you won't have the shrimp anywhere but the left side of your plate

The one who tells the truth to your face

The one who has no boundaries with you,

The one who you tell your chosen fate.

The one who laughs with you at the time that you fell

Friend I wouldn't trade you for a portable wishing well.

Photography Underrated

A moment

Frozen in time

Photography the talent

Used to warp time

To visit a memory shoved to the back of your mind

A camera your time machine

Could spend all day staring

Going back in time

To a moment perhaps lost

In the back of your mind

Photography an truly rewind time

Abstract

The colors

The shapes

Being told they must be something other than what they are

Strokes

All different

Seen as just the same

Trying to see a picture with your eyes

When you need to use your heart

The Same

We see different places

But we are all the same

All having society's

And foods with many names

Babies are always cute

And someone else is always to blame

We all have games

And the sun sky and stars we see,

Are always the same.

Cooking

It's like magic you see

But maybe a little more like chemistry

Measuring and mixing

Heating it up

Reactions going on

In the measuring cup

The only difference being

That if you eat it you probably won't throw up

Loyalty

Open

Very trusting

Empathy

Mac and Cheese

You are my Mac and Cheese

So good

So nostalgic

Reminding me of tag and truth or dare

That waft of comfort in the air

You're great for me occasionally

But not all the time

Sexism

Discrimination in plastic and color

To the young

Similarities

Those born

And those who have lived for a decade and a few

Have one thing in common

When brought outside

They want to go back in

Needing

Tears,

Joy,

Laughter,

Love,

Sadness,

And a hug

Badly

Born

When a child is born

All celebrate the birth

Except for the one being born

Bread

A loaf of bread a time

Each moment a sandwich

Some good,

Some bad

They slowly mold and crumble away

Till all you have is crumbs

Atoms

Some people are the nucleus of an atom

Always positive

Even though surrounded by negativity

Science

Amazingly

Complicated

Unbelievable

Wonderful

Frustrating

Confusing

And powerful,

All at the same time.

Butterfly

Alight on the wind

A flight in the sky

Beauty a mystery

The soft wings a disguise

Seeming very knowledgeable

In ways you can't understand

But so delicate almost seeming to break in your hand

Their time so short

But they seem to find it well spent

A delicate flower it seems

Wings of petals,

And the body a stem.

Small things

That one funny joke

The person who had on a strange coat

The casual irony occurring everyday

That one perfect time it began to rain

And the inside jokes that make you laugh like you're insane

The small things that make you grin

Are life's little wins

Arts

The scribbles on a page

The keys played and strings strummed

The hums

The brush strokes and pen lines and designs

They all have one thing in common

Emotion

They immerse you in them

Give you chills

Sadness

And feelings

Of pain

Sadness

Frustration

Love

And happiness

True art makes you feel

Trees

Tall

Old

And wrinkly

Staying in one place

Seeing all that occurred

In that one place

Watching time go on

As life goes by

Seeing

The life of all that pass by

While staying in its place

Magicians

Making what isn't there appear as if it is

Creating what seems like another being but is only ink

Creating feeling out of color and shapes

Recreating what is seen through eyes with pen and paper

Making what is nonsensical make perfect sense

And making you see through their eyes

Artists are magicians.

Oceans

Oceans

Can be many things

Churning and loud

Calming and sweet

Still and silent

Dark and eerie

Romantic and beautiful

For the ocean is a talented actor,

Who plays many roles.

Bed

The heaven you visit everyday

When work is done

And so is play

Why clean it up it will be a mess everyday

And you always wish you could stay

All day

Walking

They go and go

Right left, right left

Left right left right

One after another

Seemingly trying to beat each other

At a game that does not exist

Immersed

Stuck in between pages

Or within a screen

Immersed

In another existence

Unwilling to leave

Immersed

Away from all that matters

Never to be found again

Immersed

Taken on by a new identity

Your obsession taking over

...immersed

Subconscious

What could be there?

You don't know

What effect

You know

That eeriness

The maker of decisions you make

Who is not you

That which exists

The fear unknown

The calling unknown

All unknown

Clouds

Hopes

Seeming so great

So possible

But not stable enough to ride on

Printed in Great Britain
by Amazon